ON THE FIELD WITH . . .

PEYTON AND ELI
MANNING

MATT CHRISTOPHER®

The #1 Sports Series for Kids

ON THE FIELD WITH . . .

PEYTON AND ELI MANNING

LITTLE, BROWN AND COMPANY

New York • Boston

Little, Brown and Company

Hachette Book Group
237 Park Avenue, New York, NY 10017
Visit our Web site at www.lb-kids.com

www.mattchristopher.com

Little, Brown and Company is a division of Hachette Book Group, Inc.
The Little, Brown name and logo are trademarks of Hachette Book Group, Inc.

The publisher is not responsible for websites (or their content)
that are not owned by the publisher.

First Edition: September 2008

Matt Christopher® is a registered trademark of
Matt Christopher Royalties, Inc.

Text written by Stephanie True Peters

Library of Congress Cataloging-in-Publication Data

Christopher, Matt.
    On the field with . . . Peyton and Eli Manning / Matt Christopher.
        p. cm.— (On the field with . . .)
    ISBN 978-0-316-03696-2
1. Manning, Peyton — Juvenile literature.   2. Manning, Eli, 1981 —
Juvenile literature.   3. Football players — United States — Biography —
Juvenile literature.   4. Fathers and sons — United States —
Biography — Juvenile literature.   I. Title.
    GV939.A1C49 2008
    796.332092'2 — dc22
    [B]

                                                            2008010592

10 9 8 7

CW

Printed in the United States of America

Contents

PEYTON AND ELI MANNING

☆ PROLOGUE ☆

What Is a Dynasty?

Dictionaries describe a dynasty as an influential family that obtains and keeps power for more than one generation. Sometimes that power is political, such as that handed down from kings and queens to their children, or when the son or daughter of a government leader follows in his or her parent's footsteps. Sometimes the dynasty begins with a successful entrepreneur who passes the business on to his or her children. A dynasty can also be a family of popular actors and actresses, or musicians, or artists.

When people use the term dynasty in the sports world, usually they mean a team has had several championship years in a row. For example, the Chicago Bulls ruled the National Basketball Association from 1991 to 1998, posting six titles. The New York Yankees have had two dynastic eras, one from 1936 to 1943 and one from 1947 to 1962, racking up a grand total of 16 World Series victories. The Green

Bay Packers were untouchable from 1961 to 1967, as were the Pittsburgh Steelers from 1974 to 1979.

The sporting world has family dynasties, too, although they are not as common. After all, just because a father or a mother is a great athlete doesn't mean their children — or nieces, nephews, brothers, sisters, or other relatives — will be.

Then again, growing up with a sports star gives others in the family certain advantages. Children get an up close and personal look at how a sport is played, for one thing. They learn the finer points of the sport from a very early age and see what an athlete must do to reach the top of his or her game. Armed with this knowledge, the next generation is poised to step in when the previous one is ready to retire.

Such was the case with Major League Baseball's Ken Griffey Sr. and Ken Griffey Jr. This father-and-son duo not only excelled in the same sport, they played on the same team — and in 1990, in several of the same games, including one in which they hit back-to-back homers! (Ken Jr.'s younger brother, Craig, was also a ballplayer, although his career began and ended in the minors.)

NASCAR also has a family dynasty, the Earnhardts. The late Dale Earnhardt Sr. was one of the most popular and skillful drivers of the 1980s and

90s. His sons, Dale Jr. and Kerry, followed him into racing and have each had successful careers; his older daughter, Kelley, is Dale Jr.'s manager and business agent.

The list goes on: slugger Barry Bonds of Major League Baseball is the son of former MLB great Bobby Bonds. Muhammad Ali's daughter, Laila, is now a professional boxer, like her father. Jimmy Walker, father of NBA superstar Jalen Rose, played for three NBA teams in the 1960s and 1970s. Former National Football League tight end Don Hasselbeck is the father of two current NFL quarterbacks: Tim, of the Arizona Cardinals, and Matt, of the Seattle Seahawks.

Amazingly, the Hasselbeck trio is not the only father-son-son dynasty in the NFL currently. The other is that of the Mannings: Archie, Peyton, and Eli. This is the story of their dynasty's path to greatness.

⋆ CHAPTER ONE ⋆

1949–1967

Archie

Archie Manning, father of NFL quarterbacks Peyton and Eli, has lived in New Orleans, Louisiana, since 1971. But he doesn't consider himself as from that city.

"When anyone asks me where I'm from," he once told a reporter, "I say Drew."

"Drew" is Drew, Mississippi, a tiny, impoverished town in the northwest corner of the state, an area known as the Delta. Elisha Archibald Manning III was born there on May 19, 1949. His father, Buddy, worked for a farm machinery dealership. His mother, Sis, was a secretary for three town lawyers and "pretty much ran the town," according to Archie. Along with his older sister, Pam, they lived in a small wooden house that was actually three separate buildings that had been combined to form one dwelling.

Archie's childhood was fairly typical for the 1950s and 60s. He went to school, he did chores, he attended church and church school, and he got chocolate milk shakes at the local drugstore whenever he could. He also played sports — baseball, football, track, and basketball.

Baseball was Archie's favorite sport at first. He loved it so much, in fact, that one summer he constructed a baseball diamond between his backyard and his neighbor's so that he and his friends could play every day. "It had some lumps and bumps," Archie said of the field, "but all the measurements were correct and as far as I was concerned, it was beautiful."

Archie loved football, too. During one pickup game, the other kids made him their quarterback. After that, he never played another position if he could help it.

In the fifth grade, he joined the local peewee league. Archie remembers the terror of being a 70-pound pip-squeak facing opponents 50 pounds heavier and a few years older than him. But even the thought of being flattened by one of those boys never stopped him from playing.

"At that point I could run and throw the ball pretty well, and I hung in," he said.

Archie continued to play sports throughout his junior high and high school years. Football became

6

his favorite, despite the fact that he seemed to get injured fairly often!

One injury came when he was a freshman. The coach told him that he'd be quarterbacking an upcoming game. Archie was thrilled. But his hopes were dashed when, the very next day, he broke his right arm during practice.

That break sidelined him for the rest of the season. Fortunately, he was back in action when his sophomore year rolled around. He made the roster as the backup quarterback. By the season's last game, he had moved into the starting position.

He started his junior year, too — for three games, anyway. Then, in the midst of the third, he was crushed beneath an opponent and broke his left arm. Another break, another season of sitting on the sidelines!

Despite the injuries, Archie had played enough — and been good enough — to get noticed by a few important people that year. He didn't know that, however, until the eve of his senior year in high school. It was then that his coach told him that some college recruiters would be watching him closely in his final season. If they liked what they saw, they might offer him a scholarship.

Archie had never really considered going to college,

let alone going on a football scholarship. Still, "the more I thought about it," he said, "the more excited I got."

That excitement transferred to the field. Drew High School's football team had never been one of the area's winning teams. But in 1966, with an injury-free Archie Manning at the helm, they won five out of their ten games, the most they'd won in years.

Soon after football ended, scholarship offers from a few colleges appeared. One was from the University of Mississippi. Archie had been a longtime fan of Ole Miss, and knew that the coach, Johnny Vaught, had a reputation for developing great quarterbacks. He saw no reason not to accept their offer.

It would turn out to be a match made in heaven.

✶ CHAPTER TWO ✶

1967–1971

Manning and Ole Miss

Archie Manning began training with the Ole Miss football team in the late summer of 1967 along with seven other freshman quarterback hopefuls. Fortunately for Archie, he had a slight advantage over the others. The freshman team coach, a man named Wobble Davidson, had seen Archie quarterback the Mississippi High School All-Star game. He liked what he saw and so, when the starting players were chosen before the first practice, he chose Archie Manning as his quarterback.

Playing for the freshman team wasn't as stressful as playing for the varsity squad. There were only four games; the rest of the time was spent practicing. Such a schedule gave the freshmen time to adjust — to school, to the team, and to living away from home for the first time.

Archie went through his share of adjustments, including homesickness and faltering on the field. But slowly, he began to figure out college life, and then to enjoy it. He made friends with his fellow freshman teammates, took interesting classes, and mingled with students from a wide range of backgrounds. By the end of his freshman year, he was no longer homesick for Drew. Drew was where he had lived a happy childhood; Ole Miss was where he was learning to be an adult.

Archie spent the summer between freshman and sophomore year with one thing on his mind: what position would Coach Vaught award him when he returned in the fall?

As it turned out, he got the position that he had only dreamed about. He was going to be Ole Miss's starting quarterback!

It was unusual for a sophomore to be given that prime slot, and Archie was determined not to let Coach Vaught or the Rebel team down.

He didn't. That season, Ole Miss had a winning record of 7–3–1. One of the victories was over Virginia Tech at the Liberty Bowl in Memphis. One of the losses was the worst game in Archie's life, a 31–0 pasting by Tennessee in which he threw six interceptions.

The remainder of his sophomore year was spent studying and socializing. Archie was now a popular person on campus thanks to his position as star quarterback. No doubt, there were many young women who would have liked to know him better. But he had eyes only for one, Olivia Williams. Archie and Olivia had started dating their freshman year. They've been together ever since.

A promising college football career, a beautiful and intelligent girlfriend, a solid academic record: everything was going right for Archie as his junior year approached. Then tragedy struck the Manning family in August, when Buddy Manning died, suddenly.

In the wake of the tragedy, Manning told his mother that he wasn't going to return to Ole Miss. Money had been tight before his father's death — Buddy earned an average of $6,000 a year —and now would be even tighter. Pam was in her final year of college, and should be allowed to finish. He would return home, find a job, do *something* that would help their situation.

Sis would have none of it. She told Archie that he was going to go back to school and get his degree. He was also going to keep playing football. And she wouldn't take no for an answer.

"So I went back to Oxford," Archie said years later, "and back to football."

Back on campus, Archie threw himself into football. His junior year had many highlight moments, but the top of the list was the game against the University of Alabama on October 4, 1969. This was the first SEC game to be televised during prime-time viewing hours, and Manning wanted to be sure the fans watching at home saw a good show.

They certainly got that! He passed for a record high 436 yards and rushed for 104. Behind his dead-on throws and quick thinking, Ole Miss beat Alabama in all offensive stats — except, unfortunately, for the one that counted the most. The final score of the game was Alabama 33, Mississippi 32.

Archie continued to play good football for the remainder of the season, helping his team to a record of eight wins and three losses. For his efforts, he was named to the All-SEC (Southeastern Conference) team. He was also awarded the Mississippi Sportsman of the Year award and received the Nashville Banner Trophy as Most Valuable Player in the Southeastern Conference. To cap it all off, he came in fourth in the voting for the Heisman Trophy, a prestigious award given to the most outstanding college player of the year.

Archie was just as commanding the following season, despite being sidelined for two games with a broken left arm. The Rebels ended with a record of 7 wins, 4 losses, bringing their overall record to 22 wins, 10 losses, and 1 tie during the three years Archie started at quarterback. Once more, he was named to the All-SEC team. He also crept up the ranks in Heisman Trophy voting to number three.

Manning's college career was now behind him, but that didn't mean his life was over. In fact, some of its most important stages were just about to begin.

CHAPTER THREE

1971–1981

Manning the Saint

January 1971 was a whirlwind month for Archie Manning. On January 2, he played in his last college football game, a disappointing 35–28 loss to Auburn, at the Gator Bowl in Florida. Then he flew to Honolulu with Olivia, her parents, and his mother so that he could play in the Hula Bowl. After a week there, they all flew back to Philadelphia, Mississippi, to prepare for Archie and Olivia's wedding. The wedding took place on January 21; on January 22, the happy couple left for a five-day honeymoon.

And if that wasn't enough, on January 29, two days after they returned home, Archie was drafted by the New Orleans Saints, the second overall selection!

Manning was on cloud nine; but as his senior year came to a close, that cloud turned stormy. Archie had been drafted, but he and the Saints couldn't seem to agree on a contract. Until he was officially signed with the team, he didn't have a job. For a recent college graduate and newly married man, that was not a good position.

Fortunately, the Saints finally negotiated a contract that they and Manning could agree on: $30,000 the first year, $40,000 the second, and so on to the fifth year at $70,000, plus a $160,000 signing bonus. Archie was overjoyed, not just because the money was the most ever paid to a rookie, but because finally, he was a Saint.

He and Olivia moved to New Orleans and Archie began training with the team in preparation for his first season as a professional football player. He had his work cut out for him, to say the least.

The Saints had been at or near the bottom of the NFL pile since becoming a franchise in 1967. In those four years, they won only 14 games out of 56 played! The team hoped their record would improve with Archie Manning, one of the best college quarterbacks around, calling the shots.

In their season opener, it seemed that Archie would indeed provide the push the Saints needed to win. New Orleans played the Los Angeles Rams, a team so dominating that many were speculating they would win the championship that year. But as good as they were they wound up losing to the cellar-dwelling Saints on the last play of the game.

The Saints had reached the Rams' 3-yard line. There were four seconds left in the game and they were down by three. A field goal now would end the game in a tie (there were no overtimes in the NFL then).

But the New Orleans' coach, J.D. Roberts, told Archie to go for it. So Archie did.

"I called a run-pass option to the left," he recalled, "and I probably should have thrown, but I ran and got hit at the one-yard line and dove for the goal line, barely crossing into the end zone — where I fumbled."

Luckily for the Saints, the fumble occurred after the touchdown was complete. That victory and a second against the eventual Super Bowl champions, the Dallas Cowboys, were the most exciting wins the Saints had that season. They defeated two other teams as well to bring their total to four wins, two more than the previous season. Not a huge jump, but any improvement was better than none.

Archie's personal stats were solid, if not superlative. He completed 86 of 177 pass attempts for a total of 1,164 yards and 6 touchdowns. He added another 172 yards rushing for 4 more touchdowns.

On the downside, he also threw 9 interceptions and fumbled the ball 7 times.

In 1971, Archie had shared quarterback duties with two-year veteran Ed Hargett. In 1972, he took the helm full-time, quarterbacking every single offensive play. He rose high in the ranking in several offensive categories that season. He was first in passes completed with 230, second in yards passed with 2,781, and second in most yards passed in a single game with 198.6.

But despite his best efforts, game after game saw Archie and his teammates walking off the field in defeat. New Orleans was once again at the bottom of the pile, with a dismal 2–11–1 record in 1972.

That record didn't get much better in the following seasons, much to the disappointment of New Orleans players and fans. Even as their one shining star, Archie Manning, racked up a long list of achievements and record-breaking stats, the team as a whole struggled. They had back-to-back records of 5–9 in '73 and '74, but then dropped to 2–12 in '75.

In 1976, Archie was forced to watch his team play to a 4–10 record from the sidelines. He'd had a nagging pain in his right arm — his throwing arm — and after several examinations by different doctors, had been convinced to have the arm operated on.

He returned to the lineup the next year, with great hopes of powering on to a winning season. It was not to be. The team went 3–11.

The New Orleans Saints had now been part of the NFL for ten seasons. In that time, they had won a mere 36 games out of 140. It was understandable, then, that few people thought they'd amount to much in their 11th year.

But the Saints surprised them in 1978 by winning seven games of the newly expanded 16 scheduled. Archie's play was the main reason for their success. He had his best season ever, with 3,416 yards passing for 291 completions and 17 touchdowns. The Saints may have been third out of four in their division that year, but Archie was number one as far as the National Football Conference was concerned. They named him the NFC Most Valuable Player, the NFC Player of the Year, and the NFC Offensive MVP! He was also voted to play in the Pro Bowl for the NFC All-Stars.

The Saints were good in 1979, too, splitting the 16-game schedule with an equal number of wins and losses. Archie's stats were nearly as good as in

1978 and he made another trip to the Pro Bowl. Those fans who had once doubted their team's abilities were beginning to have hope.

Then came 1980, a year in which nothing seemed to go the Saints' way. They began the season with a 26–23 loss to the San Francisco 49ers — and then proceeded to lose the next 13 games before finally posting a victory. That win was their only one that season, for they lost their last game, too. One win, 15 losses added up to the worst record, hands down, of any team in the league.

The Saints rose slightly in the standings the following year, to 4–12, but by then New Orleans fans were so fed up with their home team that they had nicknamed them the Ain'ts. They sat in the stands of the team's new state-of-the-art arena, the Louisiana Superdome, wearing brown paper bags over their heads. And they booed, and jeered, and cursed the players, including Archie Manning.

Among those booing from the stands were two young boys, ages seven and five. That they were adding their voices to the catcalls was somewhat surprising, considering the fact that they shared a last name — not to mention a home — with the team's quarterback.

The boys' names? Cooper and Peyton Manning, Archie's sons!

Archie Manning played his last complete professional football season with the "Ain'ts" in 1981. In 1982, he came into the first game of the season for only a few plays.

Soon after that game, he received word that he had been traded mid-season to the Houston Oilers. Archie was devastated. "Leaving the Saints broke my heart," he said.

Archie played six games in an Oilers uniform, the third of three quarterbacks. He played just three games in that uniform the next year before being traded again, this time to the Minnesota Vikings.

Archie was not at all pleased to be moved so far from home. But that was the least of his worries. A few weeks into the season, he was diagnosed with Graves' disease, a condition caused by problems with the thyroid gland. He began treatments immediately, but as he reflected later, "the word retirement should then have flashed across my mind in bold letters."

Still, he recovered enough to play some games in 1984. Then, in the 1985 preseason, he had a heart-to-heart talk with his coach that finally planted the retirement seed. Once planted, it quickly took root. And so, before the start of the regular season, Archie Manning retired.

Archie Manning had had a top-notch career that was clouded by the fact that he had played for lousy teams. He was the 1978 NFC MVP, NFC Player of the Year, NFC Offensive MVP, and a two-time Pro Bowl All-Star. He received several awards, including the Byron "Whizzer" White Humanitarian Award and the Bart Starr Humanitarian Award, in recognition for his dedication to charitable causes. When the Louisiana Superdome started a tradition of putting past players on a "Wall of Fame," his was the first name up. Years after his retirement, Mississippi voted him their Greatest All-Time Athlete as well as their Most Popular Athlete of the Century.

As for his college career, Ole Miss retired his number, 18, and honored him further by making the official campus speed limit 18. He is in the National Football Foundation College Hall of Fame, and is one of the 100 All-Time Greatest College Football Players.

Was Archie upset to be leaving all this behind? Not according to him. "It was an upper instead of a downer, a plus instead of a minus," he once wrote. "Good-bye football, hello rest of my life."

Yet his retirement didn't signal a complete break with football. Far from it, for while he had hung up his helmet, his two young sons — and soon the third — were busy putting on their own.

☆ CHAPTER FOUR ☆

1974–1994

Cooper and Peyton

Olivia and Archie Manning had welcomed their first son, Cooper, in March of 1974. Peyton followed in March of 1976, and Eli in January of 1981. Each of the boys took to football like they were born to it — which, of course, they were.

Cooper and Peyton, being only two years apart, grew up playing football together. They spent hours in the Louisiana Superdome, sometimes watching their father during games, sometimes watching him during practice, and sometimes goofing around on the turf with a football. Like many brothers, they were each other's best friend — and each other's biggest rival. Archie used to say that if they could finish playing without fighting, it would be a great day for him.

Cooper, a fun-loving, athletic boy, enjoyed playing all sports but like Archie wound up concentrating on football. He started out as a quarterback but switched to wide receiver in high school when he realized catching balls suited him better than throwing them.

Archie had never pushed Cooper or his other sons into football; they chose the sport on their own. But he helped them hone their skills.

For Cooper the wide receiver, there was a drill called "Ten Passes." Cooper had to catch ten passes in a row; dropping one, even if it was the tenth, meant starting out at one again.

The hard worked paid off, however. In his junior year, Cooper caught every single pass thrown to him. He was equally successful his senior year, perhaps because he knew the new starting quarterback so well.

Like Cooper, Peyton played many sports growing up; he, too, preferred football to the rest. But unlike his brother, who was the joker of the family, Peyton was all seriousness and focus. And unlike Cooper, he liked playing quarterback.

Archie helped his younger son as he had Cooper, and believed Peyton had good football skills. Still, he didn't realize just how talented Peyton was — not right away, anyway.

Peyton and Cooper both attended Isidore Newman, a prep school in New Orleans. Peyton was named the starting quarterback his sophomore year. Cooper was the starting wide receiver. Together, they made a near-perfect pass-and-receive team, with Cooper catching 80 passes from his little brother to help Newman to a 12 and 2 record.

When Cooper enrolled at his father's alma mater, Ole Miss, after high school graduation, many people predicted that he would also follow his father into a career with the NFL. But it wasn't to be.

Cooper had been suffering from numbness in his right hand for several months before going to Ole Miss. He hadn't told anyone, not even his family, but there were hints of the problem all the same, most obviously some mysterious flubbed catches during high school games. But Cooper, being Cooper, just joked about the misses and stayed quiet.

Then, during his first game with the Rebels, that numbness reached his right leg. Cooper knew then that it was time to talk, with his family and with doctors.

The diagnosis after his examinations was frightening. Cooper had spinal stenosis, a narrowing of his spinal cavity. The doctors told him how lucky he was not to have gotten hit hard during any of his games. If he had, his spine could have been seriously injured, leaving him paralyzed.

That diagnosis ended Cooper's football career forever. As much as he loved football, he was too smart to risk his health, possibly even his life, for a sport. So he stepped off the field and took a seat in the stands, ready to cheer on his favorite players.

His brother Peyton topped that list, not only because they were family but because Peyton was good. Very, very good. In his junior year at Newman, he threw for 2,345 yards and 30 touchdowns. He was even better the following season, when he completed 168 of 265 passes for 2,703 yards and 39 touchdowns!

To few people's surprise, he was given the Gatorade Circle of Champions National Player of the Year Award that year. He was also honored by the Touchdown Club of Columbus, Ohio, as the nation's offensive player of the year and named to the All-State team.

College recruiters had been following Peyton's high school career closely. Many had expressed interest in him after his junior year. Even before his senior season, several were beating down the doors to get to him. Ole Miss was one of them. Most people thought Peyton should follow in Cooper's and Archie's footsteps and become a Rebel. In fact, Archie remembers friends telling him to convince Peyton to accept Mississippi's offer.

But Archie had never pushed any of his children toward anything. If Peyton didn't want to go to Ole Miss, that was fine with him.

Peyton didn't want to go to Ole Miss, it turned out. He wanted to go to the University of Tennessee. Why? To this day, he's not sure, just that "for some reason, Tennessee felt right."

The outcry from Ole Miss fans was loud and outraged, but it did nothing to change Peyton's mind. He had always been stubborn and his decision was made. In 1994, he would be in Tennessee to play for the Volunteers.

✭ CHAPTER FIVE ✭

1994

Peyton the Volunteer

Peyton Manning always gave one hundred percent effort to everything he did. When he wanted to learn to throw a football correctly, he asked his father how to do it. Then he practiced throwing over and over and over, until he was sure his mechanics were right.

In high school, he studied the football playbook until he knew it forward and backward. Then he executed those plays during games like a pro.

When he accepted a scholarship to Tennessee, he began taking college classes in July 1994. He didn't have to start then; he took them so that he'd be one step closer to his goal in the fall. That goal was simple: he wanted to play football for the varsity team as a freshman. When he wasn't in class, he ate, slept, and breathed football. He continued the same routine throughout preseason practices.

His single-minded focus paid off — sort of. He and

another freshman quarterback, Branndon Stewart, made the varsity roster, but with three other QBs ahead of them, they were as far down the line from the starting position as any player could be. Peyton knew it was unlikely he'd see much playing time that season, but that was okay with him. He could learn plenty by studying his team and their opponents from the sidelines, after all.

That sideline education was momentarily sidelined, however, during the first regular season game. The Volunteers were playing against the Bruins of the University of California Los Angeles in California. Peyton and Branndon were given their assignments: suit up and stand in front of the assistant coach so the other team can't see him call the plays.

Not a particularly demanding job, but Peyton took it seriously nonetheless. That's where he was when the Vols' starting quarterback, Jerry Colquitt, got hit on the seventh play of the game. Colquitt was helped off the field with a severe knee injury that wound up ending his college career.

Backup quarterback Todd Helton went in to play for Colquitt. But he couldn't make the plays happen. That's when Peyton heard something he'd never dreamed he'd hear so soon.

"All right, Peyton, you're up," David Cutcliffe, the offensive coach, said.

Peyton jogged onto the field. He was so nervous that his voice squeaked in the huddle. Then he called the play and got ready for his first drive as a college player.

They got nine yards on the first down, then nothing on the second. At third and one, Peyton hurried the snap — and paid for his haste by getting slammed to the turf by a UCLA player.

That first drive ended up being his only drive. Stewart and Helton finished off the game, a 25–23 loss for the Vols.

Peyton watched from the sidelines in the second game, but saw some play in the third. Then came the fourth match of the season.

Todd Helton was quarterbacking the game against Mississippi State. Then suddenly, *BAM!* He was hit. Hard. Like Colquitt, Helton was out for the season with a knee injury.

Peyton had never wanted to get the job of starting quarterback through injuries to his teammates. But that's what happened. He went in for Helton — and made that position his own on his third play, a whopping 76-yard touchdown throw. By game's end, he had completed 14 passes in 23 attempts for a total of

256 yards. The only thing that would have made the day sweeter was a victory, but unfortunately, Mississippi State took the game 24–21.

From that day on, Peyton never looked back. He led the Vols to seven wins as the team's starting quarterback while giving up just a single loss. One of those victories, a 31–22 win over South Carolina, saw him throwing three touchdown passes. In November, he and his teammates had back-to-back shutouts, 52–0 against Kentucky and 65–0 against Vanderbilt.

Tennessee's record was good enough to get them to the Gator Bowl, where they faced Virginia Tech. Peyton played brilliantly, completing 12 of 19 passes for 189 yards. In one play, he broke loose for a 29-yard run, helping his team to an eventual 45–23 victory. The Volunteers' head coach, Phillip Fulmer, awarded Peyton his first-ever game ball. Just as good, the SEC named him their Freshman Player of the Year.

✶ CHAPTER SIX ✶

1995–1996

Peyton the Starter

Peyton spent the rest of the year studying for classes, adding muscle to his frame, and fine-tuning his football skills. He worked on correcting a slight problem with his throw — he tended to drop the ball down too low after the snap, and then had to use valuable seconds to bring it back up into throwing position — and he studied hours and hours of football film. When the Tennessee preseason practices began in 1995, Peyton was more than ready to step into the role of starting quarterback.

From the first game to the 12th, he dominated on the field. He threw for 2,954 yards, a new school record. Out of 380 pass attempts, he completed 244 and gave up only four interceptions! He led the Vols to their best season in years, with a record of 11 wins and just one loss.

That one loss, to Florida State, was a crushing 62–37 defeat. Despite the fact that Peyton had his first 300-yard game, despite the fact that he threw two touchdowns in the first half, despite the fact that he didn't throw a single interception, they lost. "We looked absolutely unstoppable," Peyton recalled later. "But we weren't. We went into a total swoon in the second half."

Peyton battled to another 300-plus-yard game a few weeks later, in a game against Arkansas. The Razorbacks knew that the Volunteers, with a record of four wins and one loss so far, were on a roll. They were determined to stop them by blitzing Peyton time after time. But they couldn't shut him down. By game's end, he had thrown a remarkable 384 yards, completing 35 out of 46 passes to beat Arkansas 49–31. Peyton was named the SEC Player of the Week and Sporting News National Player of the Week for his effort.

The Volunteers won the rest of their games, too, and most with high scores on their side. In fact, out of all their wins, only one, against Vanderbilt, saw them scoring under 20 points. They ended their 11–1 season with a victory over Ohio State at the Citrus Bowl.

Peyton had had an absolutely fabulous year. He had surpassed the 300-yard mark in three games, set single-season school records in several categories including greatest number of passes (132) without an interception. He was named to the All-SEC first team, was a finalist for the Davey O'Brien National Quarterback Award and Football News Offensive Player of the Year, and ranked sixth in voting for the Heisman Trophy. He was no slouch off the field, either, showing the same discipline with his studies as he did with his play by earning a 3.49 grade point average (out of a 4.0), good enough to make the SEC Academic Honor Roll.

The 1996 football season started off strong, too, with Tennessee rolling over the University of Nevada, Las Vegas, 62 to 3. They won their second game as well, but faltered against Florida State, the one team that seemed capable of stopping Peyton Manning. That defeat and another late in the season were the only two the team had that year. Many of the wins saw the Vols far outscoring their opponents.

But the numbers that were really adding up were those in Peyton Manning's stats columns. His single-season total of 3,287 yards was the most ever thrown by a Tennessee quarterback. He posted another school record with 20 touchdowns. He missed tying his previous season's completion record (244 of 380) by a single completion. Another victory at the Citrus Bowl saw him carrying off the MVP award in recognition for his 408-yard passing game. And as he had the year before, Peyton won several honors for his outstanding football play as well as his top-notch academic record.

Peyton's teammates elected him to be co-captain of the squad, with Leonard Little, for the following year. But long before the season began, rumors started to fly that Manning wouldn't be there to lead. The reason was simple. The NFL had let Peyton know that if he was interested in leaving college a year early, the League was more than ready to have him.

Peyton was in a quandary. On the one hand, he had accomplished most of what he'd hoped to do at Tennessee, both academically and athletically. The lure of hundreds of thousands of dollars was strong. And what if he stayed for his final year, and wound up getting hurt? Jerry Colquitt, Todd Helton: It had happened to these teammates and countless other players. His own father had suffered injuries, although luckily none had ended his career. Joining the NFL now made sense for all those reasons.

On the other hand, he was enjoying college life. He had a good group of friends and a steady girlfriend named Ashley Thompson. If he came back, he'd be heading up one of the strongest teams in the SEC, maybe even the nation. He knew he had contributed greatly to the success of that team, but also realized that it was a solid team without him, too. If they made it to the championships without him next year, how would he feel?

With so much on the line, Peyton did what he did best: he studied the problem and talked it over with those who could help him solve it. And he sought advice from professional athletes who understood what was at stake: Troy Aikman, Drew Bledsoe, Tim Duncan, Phil Simms, Michael Jordan — and, of course, Archie Manning. Some expressed confidence that he was ready to go pro. Others told him they regretted having left college early. But only two, Jordan and his own father, said what he needed to hear.

Do what you want.

After much soul-searching, Peyton realized he wanted to go back to Tennessee. So that's what he did — much to the joy of Volunteers fans.

★ CHAPTER SEVEN ★

1997–1998

Good-bye Vols, Hello Colts!

Did returning to college end up being a wise choice? In Peyton's own words: "Nothing happened during that season to make me regret my decision."

Indeed, he had yet another superstar year. While he did throw 11 interceptions, he also had 37 touchdowns — 17 more than the year before. He surpassed his own records, completing 287 out of 477 pass attempts for an unbelievable total of 3,819 yards. In one game alone, against Kentucky, Peyton attempted 35 passes — and hit 25 of them for an amazing, record-shattering 523-yard single game total and five touchdowns!

The Volunteers roared to an 11–1 record and won the SEC title. Only the mid-season loss to the Florida Gators, their third to that team in four years, marred Peyton's final season of college football — that and the fact that he narrowly missed being awarded the Heisman Trophy.

"I'd be lying if I said I wasn't disappointed to be finishing second to Charles Woodson," Peyton said after the Heisman winner was announced. But Peyton had been raised with good manners. So instead of complaining, he congratulated Woodson, and left it at that.

Peyton did receive plenty of recognition for his outstanding play that year. He was presented with the Davey O'Brien award, given by a panel of sportswriters to their choice for the year's top quarterback. He received the Johnny Unitas Golden Arm Award, in honor of his performance as a player on the field and his citizenship and integrity off the field. He also was given the Maxwell Award, presented to the best collegiate football player by sportswriters, sportscasters, and National Collegiate Athletic Association (NCAA) coaches, and the Sullivan Award, given to the top amateur athlete in the nation.

When Peyton Manning finished at Tennessee, he left behind him a ledger full of newly minted football records. As the team's starter, he had won 39 games and lost only six. He was the school's all-time leading passer with yards (11,201), completions (851), and touchdowns (90). At draft time, he held 42 offensive records in the NCAA, SEC, and UT, plus 33 UT single game, season, and career offensive records.

That he would be the first all around pick in the up-coming NFL draft was certain.

Now all he had to do was wait to find out where he'd be going!

The answer to "Who Gets Peyton?" came in the first minutes of the 1998 NFL draft day. He had been selected by the Indianapolis Colts, a team that had gone 3–13 in 1997. The team needed inspiration and Peyton seemed like he had what they needed. He was hardworking, strong, intelligent — his college grade point average of 3.61 at graduation proved that — and most of all, he seemed eager to learn and to help.

"He's like a sponge," a coach once said of Peyton. "He wants you to give him all that you can give him."

Peyton would need to absorb as much as he could about the Colts, and quickly, too, if he was to raise his new team out of the cellar.

So he did what he'd always done. He memorized the playbook. He watched film of past games, noting problem areas and figuring out how to fix them. He worked out with weights, ran to improve his speed, and drilled to increase his dexterity. He spent hours practicing with Colts receivers, like Marvin Harrison, perfecting the timing of patterns and just getting to know his fellow teammates.

"It's gotten to the point where he looks at me and I know the ball is coming," Harrison once commented.

Unfortunately, all of Peyton's hard work didn't pay off for the team right away. The Colts dropped their first four games before finally defeating the San Diego Chargers 17–12 in the beginning of October. That win was followed by four more losses, to give the Colts a dismal 1–8 record by mid-November!

Manning had posted some decent stats, including near or above 50 percent in pass completion to attempts. But he'd also thrown 18 interceptions in nine games. Where was the Peyton Manning Colts fans had hoped would lead their team to triumph?

He turned up in full force in the final seconds at end of the November 15 game against the New York Jets.

The Jets had won four in a row and had trounced the Colts earlier in the season 44–6. Now they were in the lead 23–17 with less than three minutes left to play. The Colts had possession at their own 38-yard line. It was fourth down, with 15 yards to go. Manning got the word: the Colts were going to try to make first down.

A pass was the only possible answer. Manning took the snap, faded back into the pocket, and looked for the open receiver. He saw running back Kevin Faulk in the clear. He threw. Faulk caught the ball for an 18-yard gain — and a first down!

Peyton wasn't done yet. He marched the team slowly but surely down the field and deep into Jets territory. Then, with a mere 52 seconds left on the clock, he found Marvin Harrison at the Jets' 14-yard line.

The Colts were now within striking range. But would they be able to capitalize on the opportunity? It didn't seem so on the next play, an incompletion aimed at tight end Ken Dilger. There were now only 24 seconds remaining.

Once more, Peyton went to the pass. With his front line giving him the time he needed, he bulleted a pass to Marcus Pollard. Pollard gathered it in at the 3-yard line and then fought his way over the goal line. Touchdown! The game was tied and when the extra point kick was good, the Colts had their second win of the season, thanks to an incredible 80-yard, 15-play drive by rookie Peyton Manning.

The Colts added only one other victory in 1998 to end their season 3–13 for the second year in a row. Yet in the midst of that dismal record was a glimmer of hope: Peyton Manning.

Archie's son had posted absolutely phenomenal

numbers. He started all 16 games and took every single snap. He threw 326 completions in 575 attempts for a total of 3,739 yards. And while it was true that he had his highest number of interceptions in a single season ever with 28, he also threw for 26 touchdowns.

He had four games of 300 yards or more, the most of any rookie ever and good enough to tie Hall of Famer Johnny Unitas's single-season record. On December 6, he broke a 50-year-old rookie record when he threw a touchdown pass in his tenth straight game. Two weeks later, he broke three other long-standing records, for greatest number of completions in a season (309, besting Jeff George's 1991 record of 292); yards passing (3,514, besting Unitas' 1963 record of 3,481); and touchdown passes in consecutive games (14, besting Earl Morrall's 13 in 1968).

But like the true team player that he is, Peyton would have traded those record-breaking moments for even one more hash mark in the Colts "win" column.

★ CHAPTER EIGHT ★

1998–2002

Peyton in Charge

Peyton Manning did his best to put the season's disappointments behind him, and to follow pro football quarterback Troy Aikman's advice to not throw a football until the spring so that his arm and shoulder could get plenty of rest.

But resting and relaxing were not part of Peyton's makeup. Figuring out what had gone wrong and doing everything possible to fix it was. So, as usual, Peyton spent the off-season working out, studying film, and perfecting as many aspects of his game as he could. When the 1999 season began, he was more than ready.

The Colts were ready, too. They had added a hot new player to their offense, a running back named Edgerrin James. Talented wide receiver Marvin Harrison, whom Peyton had found for nearly 800 yards the previous year, returned to the lineup, too.

Individually, Manning, James, and Harrison had great talent. Only time would tell if they could mesh their skills well enough to win games.

The Colts' first game was against the Buffalo Bills on September 12. The Bills had had a good year in 1998, including two decisive wins over the Colts. This outing, however, ended differently. With the teams of Manning to Harrison and Manning to James, the Colts out-passed and out-rushed the Bills to win 31 to 14.

Indianapolis fans were pleased, but of course, it was just one game. When the Colts lost two of their next three, it seemed the team was on course for yet another season in the cellar.

Then something happened. The Colts won, and they kept winning, game after game after game until in all, they took 11 in a row! Their final game, to the Bills, was a loss, but few people cared. Indianapolis had reversed their last-place record from 3–13 to claim first-place honors and the AFC East title with 13–3! Harrison had caught a total of 115 passes from Manning for 1,663 yards. James had nearly 2,140 yards combined rushing and receiving. It was only the second time in NFL history that a team's rushing-receiving had exceeded 1,500 yards.

Together, the threesome had combined for 29 of the team's 46 touchdowns!

It was the Colts' best season since the 1960s and good enough to send them to the playoffs. Unfortunately, they fell in the first round to the Tennessee Titans, 19–16.

Not surprisingly, Manning was selected to play in the Pro Bowl (the NFL's All-Star game) that year, the first of many times he would be chosen — and accept. He completed 17 of 24 pass attempts that game to help his side to a decisive 51–31 victory.

After such a stellar turnaround season in 1999, the Colts entered the 2000 season as the favorites to win the AFC East division. Many predicted they would reach the Super Bowl. But it was not to be.

While the offense played well, with Manning, James, and Harrison posting their second consecutive 4,000-1,000-1,000-yard season — a first for an offensive trio in NFL history — the team's defense seemed to fall apart in mid-season. Indianapolis ended with 10–6. That was good enough for a wild-card berth in the playoffs, but sadly, the team lost in the first game to Miami in overtime.

Things went from bad to worse in 2001, when

the Colts reversed their record from 10–6 to 6–10.
They reversed that record again in 2002, thanks
in large part to a record-breaking year from Peyton. He became the first quarterback in NFL
history to start a career with five consecutive seasons
of 3,000 or more passing yards. He was also the
first to post 4,000 passing yards for four seasons in
a row.

Still, the team suffered with a lackluster defense
and seemingly careless offense. Peyton was far from
blameless, throwing a whopping 59 interceptions
from 2000 to 2002. But far and away his worst game
of the season — perhaps one of his worst ever —
came in the Colts' 2002 postseason outing.

Indianapolis had squeaked into the playoffs after
besting the Jacksonville Jaguars 20–13 in the last
game of the regular season. They had won that
game in the final three minutes, with a 47-yard
drive in seven plays that ended with an 11-yard
touchdown pass from Peyton to Marcus Pollard.

"That was probably one of our biggest plays of the
year," Manning said after the game.

As it turned out, it was also their last big play of
the year. The Colts were crushed by the New York
Jets one week later when, for the first time since

Peyton had joined the team, Indianapolis failed to score a single point.

Peyton felt personally responsible for the offense's breakdown. "Not a whole lot went right," he said, adding that after such a demoralizing defeat, it was going to be a long off-season.

✶ CHAPTER NINE ✶

2003–2005

Near-Perfect Peyton

The Colts had now had three trips to the playoffs with Peyton Manning at the helm. They hadn't advanced beyond the first round any of those times. But Manning hadn't given up hope of leading his team not just to the postseason, but all the way to the Super Bowl.

And in 2003, he got them close — very, very close. Indianapolis went 12–4 that season, their best record in four years. One of those wins stands out as one of the most dominant of Peyton's career.

The Colts were playing the New Orleans Saints. Peyton took to the field in the Superdome — the field where he and Cooper had often played catch as children — and proceeded to absolutely demolish the team his father had once quarterbacked.

The rout began early, in the first two minutes of the first quarter. The Saints received the opening kickoff. On the second play of the game, the Colts intercepted a pass!

The Colts' offense hurried onto the field to set up at the Saints' 23-yard line. The first play went nowhere, but the second, a pass from Manning to Harrison, gained Indianapolis six yards.

Now it was third and four at New Orleans's 17-yard line. Manning took the snap, faded back, and found running back Ricky Williams in the end zone. Touchdown!

Six minutes later, the Colts scored again, this time on a 61-yard, eight-play drive that ended with a 14-yard pass from Manning into the hands of Marvin Harrison.

Harrison was the receiver of yet another touchdown pass in the second quarter, this one an incredible 79-yard spiraling bomb. With all three extra-point kicks going through the uprights, the Colts were up 21–0. Each team added a field goal and when the Saints posted a touchdown, the gap closed to 24–10 at the half.

It didn't stay that way for long. Amazingly, the Colts *doubled* their points to 48 in the third quarter, with a field goal and three touchdowns. Those three TDs, all made on passes, brought Manning's game total to six — the most ever scored by a Colt quarterback in a single game. Indianapolis won the game 55–21.

The Colts didn't chalk up that many points again in 2003, but they earned a wild-card slot in the playoffs. Now the question on everyone's mind was, would Indianapolis finally be able to win a postseason game?

The Colts answered that question with a resounding YES in their meeting with the Denver Broncos on January 4. Peyton was masterful in the pocket. Three minutes into the game he rifled a 31-yard pass to wide receiver Brandon Stokley in the end zone for six points. Then, with 30 seconds remaining in the first quarter, he drilled another pass, this one from 46 yards out, to Marvin Harrison, for another touchdown.

In their first possession in the second quarter, *bam!* Peyton hit Harrison with yet another touchdown pass. And then, with two minutes remaining in the half, he spiraled the ball 87 long yards into Stokley's waiting hands for a fourth TD.

Four touchdowns, four extra points, plus a field goal gave the Colts 31 points. The Broncos only had 3 points.

Denver eventually managed to make it into the

end zone for six points early in the fourth quarter. But by then, it was far too late to matter. Indianapolis had steamrolled over them for a fifth touchdown to bring their grand total to 41 points.

Stokley summed up the reason for the overwhelming victory with a simple observation: "Every ball [Manning] threw was perfect."

Indeed they were. Peyton ended the game with a perfect passer rating of 158.3 (a figure calculated using the quarterback's passing stats), his fourth time achieving this percentage. He threw touchdown passes on each of the Colts' first four possessions, and was 20 for 26 for 377 yards total.

Thanks to Peyton's amazing performance, the Colts moved on to the next round of the playoffs. He had finally proven that he could hold his own during a big game — but many wondered if he could do it again.

He could, and did, big-time, in the following week's 38–31 win against the Kansas City Chiefs. Peyton picked apart the Chiefs' defense to march the Colts down the field and onto the scoreboard in six of their first seven possessions. His command of the field was so overpowering that even the Chiefs were in awe.

"He is the master," said Eric Hicks, defensive end

for Kansas City. "That was an amazing performance. I never would have thought a quarterback would play two games in a row like that."

Unfortunately for Indianapolis fans, those two games would not stretch into three. The next week the Colts fell to the New England Patriots in Foxboro, Massachusetts. After his last two incredible performances, Manning seemed unable to find his rhythm. He threw just one touchdown pass — and four interceptions, the most he'd thrown in a single game since 2001.

"I just made some bad throws, some bad decisions," Peyton admitted after the game. Showing good sportsmanship, he also commented that he thought the Patriots and their star quarterback, Tom Brady, had played very well. New England went on to win their second Super Bowl in three years.

Indianapolis faced New England again in their 2004 season opener — and again, they lost despite having drawn within striking distance in the last four minutes of the game. While Brady surpassed Peyton in all passing categories that game, Manning did hit a career milestone by reaching 25,000 yards passing. He had done it in 95 games, the second fastest of any quarterback. Only Dan Marino got there sooner, in 92 games.

The Colts won their next four games, dropped two in a row, and then roared through the final weeks with eight victories. Six of those games had Indianapolis scoring 30 or more points, and four were 40 or more. Those four were won in a row, making Indianapolis only the third team in NFL history to score 40 or higher in four consecutive outings.

"We've been on a hot streak," Manning commented with a smile after one win.

The last win, against the San Diego Chargers, was a particularly hard-fought battle. The Colts were down by 15 in the fourth quarter. Manning had been having a painful day, getting sacked four times and forced to fumble twice. He threw some terrible passes, too, something he so rarely did. With the way their quarterback was playing, it seemed all but impossible for Indianapolis to pull out a win.

Then the Colts got lucky. Dominic Rhodes returned the kickoff nearly the entire length of the field for a touchdown to close the gap from 31–16 to 31–22. The extra point bumped them up one closer.

The score stayed at 31–23 for the next several minutes. Then the Colts took possession on their own 20-yard line with 3:42 remaining. One incomplete pass and one sack later, they had been pushed back to their own 15.

Fans started leaving the stands, certain that the Chargers had won, for how in the world could the Colts possibly take it away now?

How? Simple: Peyton Manning. First came an 11-yard completion to Edgerrin James, then another pass for a gain of 19 yards. Three more passes chewed up 34 more yards of the field and suddenly, it was first and ten at the Chargers' 21-yard line!

Peyton had four tries to work the ball into the end zone. He only needed one. He took the snap, faded back, saw Stokley in the clear, and threw. Stokley gathered it in for six!

The Colts were now down by two. There was less than a minute remaining in the game. Everyone knew what they had to do — go for a two-point conversion to send the game into overtime. Manning called a draw play for James. The team lined up quickly. Then, like a well-oiled machine, the ball went from the center to Manning to James, who bulled his way into the end zone to tie the game!

Going into overtime, the Colts had all the momentum. They marched into field goal range in just five plays. One kick later, they had their 12th victory of the year.

The win was particularly sweet for Manning because with that final touchdown pass, he vaulted over Dan Marino to become the first NFL player in history to make 49 TD passes in a single season. Manning also surpassed quarterback Steve Young's 1994 top passer rating, finishing with 121.1 to Young's 112.8.

The season ended with a disappointing loss, but in all, the Colts had a 12–4 record, good enough to clinch the wild-card slot in the playoffs. They won that first game by a wide margin, 49–24, over the Denver Broncos.

But when Indianapolis met the New England Patriots in the next round, the end result was quite different. The Colts, one of the highest scoring offenses in the league in years, were held to just one field goal.

"It was an excellent run, a fine year," Manning said after the defeat. Then he added, "Eventually, it will be our time."

That time seemed on the verge of happening in 2005. The Indianapolis Colts galloped their way through the regular season, winning their first 13 games before falling to the San Diego Chargers. Their final record of 14–2 was a franchise best and the best in their division.

Most football watchers believed Indianapolis would finally win the Super Bowl that year. But the team had to make it through the playoff games first. Unfortunately for Colts fans, the curse that had haunted their team in postseasons past returned. Indianapolis lost to the Pittsburgh Steelers when a 46-yard game-tying field goal attempt by the Colts kicker Mike Vanderjagt flew wide of the uprights.

The devastating loss ended the Colts' Super Bowl run for that year. But what a year it had been for the team, particularly for their offense. Peyton reached the 30,000-yard passing milestone in his 115th game, making him second only to Dan Marino, who had reached it in 114 games. He and receiver Marvin Harrison set a joint league record by completing 9,568 passing yards, the most ever by a quarterback-receiver duo. They topped another famous QB-WR duo, Steve Young and Jerry Rice, with the most touchdowns (86).

Such records were great, of course — but they were much, much better when they added up to a shot at the Super Bowl. That's what Peyton set his sights on for the coming season.

Archie Manning, father of Peyton, Cooper, and Eli, was a great quarterback in his day. Here, he throws a pass to one of his team-mates on the New Orleans Saints.

Peyton Manning blew away several school records as quarterback for the Volunteers of the University of Tennessee.

Eli Manning was a star at Ole Miss, just as his father was thirty years earlier. Eli broke many of Archie's long-standing school records.

Eli is on the lookout for an open receiver.

Peyton Manning is seen here in 1998, his rookie year, when he crushed several single season records.

Peyton Manning, the MVP of Super Bowl XLI, grins happily while holding the Vince Lombardi Trophy.

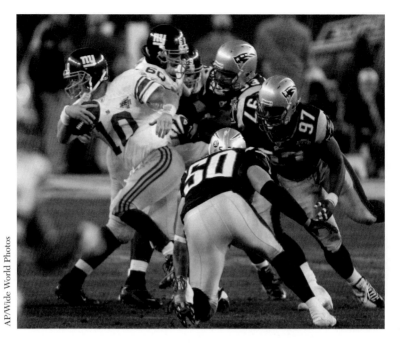

Eli scrambles free in the final minute of the fourth quarter of Super Bowl XLII—and gets off the pass that sets up the game-winning touchdown!

The Manning dynasty: Archie, Eli, and Peyton.

★ CHAPTER TEN ★

2006

Peyton's Super Season

The 2006 Indianapolis Colts were almost, but not quite, as dominant as the 2005 team had been. They started the season 9–0 then dropped four of their last seven for a record of 12–4. Their last victory, the one that edged them into the postseason, was due in large part to an unusual move by Peyton Manning.

The Colts were playing the Miami Dolphins. The Dolphins were 6–9, out of playoff contention, but that didn't mean they weren't playing to win.

The Dolphins drew first blood with an early field goal. But the Colts answered with a touchdown. Miami came within one after another field goal. Then Manning drove his team down the field, from their own 20 to the Dolphins' 11, in six plays.

With 26 seconds left in the first quarter, Peyton took the snap and looked for an open man to pass to. He didn't see anyone. But he did see something else: a hole in the defense. Instinct took over. He scrambled through that hole and into the end zone. Touchdown!

The game ended with a final score of 27–22 Colts. If not for Manning's scramble, it might very well have been Dolphins 22–Colts 20.

In the first game in the postseason, however, it was the Indianapolis defense that won the day, and the game. Peyton gave them full credit for the 23–8 victory over the Chiefs and in the same breath acknowledged fully that he had not played well. "Our defense was awesome today," he said. "We made some mistakes and the defense made sure we didn't pay for it."

There would be no room for mistakes in the next game, against the very powerful Baltimore Ravens. But once more, Peyton did not look like the record-breaking quarterback he was. Time and again, he fell short of getting the ball into the end zone.

For once, however, it didn't matter. In a strange, game-long battle-of-the-kickers, all the points on the both sides of the scoreboard came from field goals. Luckily for the Colts, their superstar kicker, Adam Vinatieri, chalked up five for 15 points, while the Ravens' kicker only boosted two through the posts.

Indianapolis now faced their arch-nemesis, the New England Patriots, for the AFC title and the chance at the Super Bowl. Peyton Manning and the Colts were 0–2 in the postseason against Tom Brady and the Pats. No one on the Indianapolis team wanted to see that record go to 0–3.

The game started out tense for the Colts, however, with the Pats getting on the board with a touchdown midway through the first quarter. Vinatieri booted a field goal at the close of the quarter, but Manning and the Colts knew that this game, unlike the last, would be decided by seven-point touchdowns, not three-point field goals. They had to get the ball into the end zone or else watch New England roll over them to the Super Bowl again.

But field goals were all the Colts seemed capable of getting. By halftime, they had a measly 6 points. The Patriots, meanwhile, had 21.

Then something happened. Indianapolis started to chip away at New England's lead. Manning led the charge in their first possession in the third quarter, inching his team into New England territory slowly but surely to land them on the Patriots' 1-yard line.

It was third down. Manning took the snap. Without hesitation, he put his head down and bulled his way over the line. Touchdown! The extra kick was good. The score was Pats 21, Colts 13.

Indianapolis's offense hurried off the field to make way for the defense. Three plays later, they switched again after the Colts' defense completely shut down Tom Brady.

Manning fired off a 25-yard pass into the waiting hands of Dallas Clark. Then he handed off to Dominic Rhodes who ate up 19 more yards. Eight more yards plus an additional ten on Patriot penalties put the Colts at the 1-yard line again — and again they scored a touchdown! They went for the two-point conversion rather than the extra point and when they made it, the score was tied.

Indianapolis fans were going crazy. They quieted a few minutes later, however, when the Patriots added another seven to their side — only to roar to life once more when the Colts recovered their own fumble just inside New England's end zone!

Tie game, 28–28. The Pats booted a field goal to make it 31–28. The Colts kicked one of their own. Tie game, 31–31. Then another Patriots field goal boosted them to a three-point lead with less than four minutes remaining in the game.

The clock ticked down. The teams traded possessions but neither made anything happen.

With 2:17 left on the clock, the Colts got the ball on their own 20-yard line. Two minutes and 17 seconds may not seem like a lot of time, but it was more than enough for Peyton Manning to work his team right where he wanted them: in front of New England's goal posts. Manning handed off to Joseph Addai. Addai put his shoulder down and barreled through the defense and into the end zone! Touchdown! The Colts took the lead for the first time all game!

There was one minute left. Tom Brady raced onto the field with his offense and began barking out signals.

Peyton Manning sat on the bench. He bowed his head, too nervous to watch. He knew how good Brady was. There was every possibility that the New England quarterback would do just what he himself had just done — that is, score in a minute.

Brady's first pass was incomplete. His second went for 19 yards. His third was good for 15 more. Then, with 24 seconds remaining, he launched another pass aimed at the waiting hands of Troy Brown.

The ball never reached Brown because Marlin Jackson of the Colts intercepted it! Indianapolis's offense raced onto the field. Manning took the snap. The second the ball hit his hands, he knelt down. The clock ran out. The Colts were going to the Super Bowl!

Manning tore off his helmet with a whoop. "I don't know if you're supposed to pray for stuff like that," he said later, "but I said a little prayer."

It had taken Peyton Manning nine years, but he had finally brought his team to the Super Bowl. The Colts were favored to beat the NFC champs, the Chicago Bears, but no one knew better than Peyton how wrong predictions could be.

★ CHAPTER ELEVEN ★

2007

A Soggy Super Bowl

Super Bowl XLI took place on February 4, 2007, in Miami's stadium. Kickoff was at 6:25 PM — and a soggy kickoff it was, too. The game started in the midst of a downpour, marking the first time in NFL history that the Super Bowl was played in the rain.

The Bears won the toss and elected to receive. Adam Vinatieri lofted a 62-yard kick. Devin Hester got under it, caught it, and began to run. He ran — and ran — and ran, a total of 92 yards, from Chicago's 8-yard line all the way to Indianapolis's end zone for a touchdown! The game clock had ticked off less than 30 seconds, and the Bears were already up, 7–0!

The Colts were shocked. But Peyton shook it off. There was a whole game yet to be played, after all, plenty of time to overcome a mere seven points. All Indianapolis needed to do was play the kind of heads-up ball they'd been playing throughout the postseason.

But they didn't — not at first, anyway. On their initial possession, they committed two penalties that cost them ten yards. Manning threw two incomplete passes and then an interception!

The Bears took over. Fortunately, the Colts' defense stopped them cold. The offense took over at their own 20-yard line. By then, Manning seemed to be settling down. More importantly, he seemed to be figuring out the Bears' defense and how to deal with the wet conditions.

He handed off to Joseph Addai twice for a gain of eight yards. Then he threw a short pass to Marvin Harrison for seven more and first down. Another short pass, this time to Addai, chewed up five more yards. Then Addai rushed for a gain of one and Dallas Clark nabbed a pass to the left for six.

The Colts were now three yards away from the 50-yard line. Addai was stopped on the next rush. Manning's pass attempt was incomplete. It was third and ten on Indianapolis' 47-yard line. If the next play failed, they would have to punt.

The next play didn't fail. Peyton called the signals, dropped back into the pocket, and unleashed a long bomb moments before Tank Johnson of the Bears reached him for the tackle. The ball spiraled through the driving rain and started down toward the waiting hands of Reggie Wayne. Wayne stretched up, caught the slippery ball, and danced into the end zone! Touchdown!

What happened in the next few plays was the stuff of sports blooper videos.

First, the ball slipped out of Hunter Smith's hands when he tried to set it for Adam Vinatieri's extra point kick. Vinatieri had nothing to kick, so the Colts' score stayed at six instead of going to seven.

The Colts' kickoff went smoothly but then, after returning the ball nine yards, the Bears' tight end Gabe Reid fumbled. Colts guard Dylan Gandy scooped up the ball and ran for three in the opposite direction before being tackled. The Colts had regained possession at Chicago's 34-yard line!

Getting a touchdown from so close should have been a cakewalk for Manning and the Colts. But on the first snap, Peyton fumbled — and Chicago recovered at their own 41-yard line! The Bears took full advantage of the turnover by scoring their second touchdown of the game to make it Chicago 14, Indianapolis 6 at the end of the quarter.

A bobbled snap and two fumbles? Anyone who hadn't figured out that the rain was going to be a factor in this game sure knew it now!

Indianapolis started off the second quarter with an early field goal to pull within five of the Bears. On the Colts' next possession, Peyton took three minutes to drive the team 58 yards — and into the end zone for a touchdown. This time, the extra point was good and the Colts had their first lead of the game, 16–14.

That was the score going into the third quarter. Indianapolis received the kick and proceeded to slowly move down the field. Twice Peyton slipped and fell while throwing — but both times, he got the passes off, and both times, they were complete. After more than seven minutes and a combination of short passes and rush plays, the Colts were knocking on the door to the Bears' end zone. But the Bears turned them away, so the Colts settled for a field goal instead of a touchdown.

Vinatieri kicked another field goal four minutes later, bringing the score to Colts 22, Bears 14. Then Chicago's kicker booted one of his own to bring the Bears to within five points of the Colts with one minute left in the quarter.

Five points is easy to overcome. All a team needs

to do is get a single touchdown. And Chicago came close to doing just that — only to see their hopes dashed when a long pass from quarterback Rex Grossman ended up in the hands of Colt Kelvin Hayden. Hayden then ran the ball the length of the field into the end zone for an Indianapolis touchdown.

That interception was the final nail in the Bears' coffin. At the final buzzer, the score stood at Colts 29, Bears 17. Indianapolis had won its first Super Bowl!

Thanks to the constant rain, Super Bowl XLI was destined to go down as the sloppiest championship played in the NFL's history. But the wet conditions couldn't put a damper on the joy felt by Peyton Manning and the Colts as they swarmed the field in victory.

In the center of the celebration, Colts' coach Tony Dungy, the first African-American head coach to win a Super Bowl, grabbed Manning and hugged him. Soon afterward, the announcement was made that Peyton was the game's MVP. He was proud to win that award, but quickly deflected personal congratulations. Instead, he made sure everyone knew the day's victory belonged to the team.

"I love this being a team win, because that's what we've done all season," he said. "We just kept chipping away at it and getting some points.

"It's hard to put into words," he added. "I'm proud

to be part of this team. We stuck together, won this game for our leader, Tony Dungy."

Peyton took to the podium alongside Dungy and team president Bill Polian and, before a crowd of cheering fans, held the Vince Lombardi Trophy aloft for all to see — including those who meant the most to him: his father, Archie; his mother, Olivia; his brothers Cooper and Eli; and his wife, Ashley, all of whom were at the game and celebrated his victory with him.

Little did they know that just one year later, they would all be celebrating another Super Bowl win. But this time, it would be a different Manning who stood at center stage.

⋆ CHAPTER TWELVE ⋆

1981–1999

Eli's Turn

"Watch out, world. [Eli is] the best one."

Eli Manning was only thirteen years old when his brother Peyton wrote those words in his senior high school yearbook. It would be two years before he could even try out for the Isidore Newman football team.

But Peyton believed that when the time came, his little brother would surpass everything he had accomplished in high school — and maybe even beyond.

Eli Manning was born five years after Peyton and seven years after Cooper. When Eli was a toddler, Archie was traveling a great deal and his brothers were in school. Therefore, Eli formed a strong bond with his mother. He was like Olivia in many ways — calm in a crisis, easygoing, and quiet. According to his brothers and parents, nothing ever really seemed to faze Eli. Unlike Cooper and Peyton, whose competitiveness was well known early on, Eli didn't appear to care if he won or lost. That carefree attitude earned him a nickname: Easy.

Perhaps that's why Peyton, then in college, was so shocked when Eli, then in high school, dunked over him during a friendly game of one-on-one basketball.

"I always thought of him as being just this neat kid," Peyton admitted, "as nice as could be, saying 'Yes, sir' and 'No, sir' to everybody and never causing me any problems the way I did Cooper."

Eli, it turned out, was every bit as competitive as his brothers — he just didn't show it. In fact, Cooper thought his youngest brother was downright emotionless. Not showing emotion in normal, day-to-day life was okay, but not when it came to the world of sports. There, Cooper felt, his brother needed to demonstrate that he cared about the game he was playing. "If you can't feel it," he once admonished Eli, "at least fake it!"

But emotional outbursts simply weren't Eli's way. Instead, when it came to sports, he was the human embodiment of the phrase "still waters run deep." On the surface, he appeared to be unconcerned, or "still." But deep down inside, he was thinking long and hard about the game, planning his next move, or next three, with one goal in mind: to win.

Like his older brothers, Eli took to sports at an early age. Football, of course, but he also played basketball and baseball. He played them all very well, yet never bragged about his achievements. He didn't play to get attention or glory. He played because he loved to play.

Like Peyton and Cooper, Eli attended Isidore Newman High School. He made the football team as a freshman, as the backup quarterback. He also started some games. When he didn't start, he seemed content to watch from the sidelines.

Eli was named the school's starting quarterback as a sophomore, just as Peyton had been five years earlier. And like Peyton, he racked up incredible numbers in the position that year, including 139 completions out of 245 pass attempts for 22 touchdowns. Behind his precision throwing, the team went 8–2, good enough for a spot in the state playoffs. They lost in the first round, but for his efforts, Eli was named to the All-State team.

Eli improved the team's record the following year to 9–1. Isidore Newman made it to the playoffs again, and this time they went all way to the finals before being beaten. And Eli's senior year, Newman ended with an 11–1 record and a third year in the playoffs, where they reached the state quarterfinals.

Eli ended his high school career with numbers and awards that rivaled those of his famous older brother. He was named All-American, All-State, and All-District, was the *USA Today* Player of the Year in Louisiana, All-Metro MVP, and the seventh-ranked Super Prep Louisiana Top 38. In four years, he completed 429 of 725 passes, for a grand total of 7,389 yards and 81 touchdowns — 200 more yards than Peyton's high school total, but three fewer touchdowns.

To say that the top football colleges in the nation were knocking on Eli's door was an understatement. They were pounding, hammering, and beating on every part of the Manning house!

Eli reacted to the furor over him in his usual way. He was quiet. He kept his thoughts about the various offers to himself. And then, when he was ready, he told his mother and father where he had decided to go in the simplest way possible: "Oh. Ole Miss, of course."

⋆ CHAPTER THIRTEEN ⋆

1999–2001

Another Manning at Ole Miss

Archie and Olivia Manning were delighted that Eli had chosen to attend the University of Mississippi. Cooper, an Ole Miss alum, was also pleased. Even Peyton, the one Manning who hadn't attended Mississippi, was happy because Eli would be coached by a man Peyton had great respect for, David Cutcliffe. Coach Cut, as the middle Manning called him, had been Peyton's offensive coach at Tennessee and had just been named to the head coach position at Ole Miss. Peyton had learned a great deal from him and believed Eli would, too.

Eli announced his decision to the football world with a ten-minute prepared speech before a captive audience of television and radio crews. At the very end, he answered the unspoken question most of them probably would have asked. "This really didn't have anything to do with my father playing at Ole Miss. That was over thirty years ago."

Eli didn't mean any disrespect; he just wanted to be sure everyone knew that he and Archie were two different players. In fact, when the college offered to "unretire" Archie's number 18 for Eli to wear, Eli turned them down and chose number 10 instead.

Eli began at Mississippi in the fall of 1999. He was on the football team, of course, but was red-shirted for the season, meaning he would practice with the Rebels but not play in competition.

Red-shirting is a common practice in college athletics. It gives hot prospects like Eli the opportunity to hone their skills with their team, to learn the plays, and to get to know their teammates' strengths and weaknesses. Then, when they take to the field the following year, they are ready — and have four years of playing ahead of them.

If Eli was disappointed to be red-shirted, he didn't show it. Instead, he took the time to learn all he could during practices. He also settled into college life and into his academic studies. He did so well in the latter that he made the Chancellor's Honor Roll that fall.

Eli worked out with the team throughout the spring and summer of 2000, and went into the football season that fall knowing that he'd be playing backup quarterback to senior Romaro Miller. As backup, he spent most games on the bench watching as Miller drove the Rebels to a 7–5 season. That record was good enough to earn them a spot in the Music City Bowl, against West Virginia.

The Rebels hoped to end their season on a high note, but unfortunately it was not to be. The Mountaineers pounded them in the first three quarters, going up 49–9 at one point. The Rebels needed someone to inspire them to play better ball if they were going to leave the game with their dignity intact.

That someone turned out to be Eli Manning. With the score 49–16 in the fourth quarter, Coach Cutcliffe put Eli in — and he began to work magic. In six and a half minutes, he threw three touchdown passes to tighten the score to 49–38!

It was an heroic effort, but wound up being just too late in the game. Eli was philosophical afterward. "I wasn't really expecting a comeback," he said. "I was just trying to score of couple of points."

The loss was a disappointment for the Rebels but they had reason to hope nonetheless. With Miller graduating, Eli would start as their quarterback the following season. If he was as effective then as he had been at the Music City Bowl, they would have a very strong season.

At first, it looked like their hopes were well-founded. Manning started in his first college game on September 1, 2001, against Murray State — and what a start it was! He threw 23 passes, 20 of which were completions, for a total of 271 yards. He set a school record with five touchdown passes. Four of those touchdowns came in the first half alone, two in the first quarter. With the Rebs' final touchdown coming on an amazing — and no doubt demoralizing, for Murray — 93-yard kickoff return, the score ended at Ole Miss 49, Murray State 14.

With Eli at the helm, the Rebels won five of their next six games. Then came the longest battle in college football history to date.

The Ole Miss Rebels were facing the Arkansas Razorbacks at home on November 3, 2001. Kickoff was at 7:00 PM. Four and a half hours and seven overtimes later, the game finally ended!

Ole Miss drew first blood with a one-yard run into the end zone and extra point kick for seven on the scoreboard. The Razorbacks answered those seven with seven of their own in the second quarter.

It was a tie ball game going into the second half — and was still tied going into the fourth quarter, thanks to field goals by both sides. Then in the fourth quarter, Arkansas pulled ahead on a two-yard touchdown run and extra-point kick.

The game might have ended then, with the score 17–10 in favor of the Razorbacks. But Eli Manning worked his team down the field, into touchdown range, and then into the end zone to tie it all up again with five minutes remaining. When Arkansas failed to score on their final possession, the game went into overtime.

That's when the scoring took off into the stratosphere. First the Razorbacks ran the ball 16 yards for a touchdown to go up by seven. Then the Rebels returned the favor with a touchdown of their own on an 11-yard pass from Eli Manning to Jason Armstead. Tie game, 24–24.

Both teams scored six more. Both failed in their two-point conversion attempts. 30–30. Ole Miss took the lead after that, with a beautiful 21-yard pass from Manning to freshman wide receiver Bill Flowers. Again, their attempted two-point conversion went nowhere, as did the Razorbacks' after their touchdown.

The score was 36–36. Then it was 42–36, Arkansas. Ole Miss evened it up again with Eli's third overtime touchdown pass, his fourth for the game. Eli threw yet another touchdown pass, this one from 15 yards, to give the Rebels the jump on the Razorbacks. When their two-point conversion attempt succeeded, they were up by eight.

The teams were now deep into their sixth overtime. If the Rebels could hold off the Razorbacks for a few minutes longer, they would take the game.

They didn't. Arkansas tied it up with a two-yard run and a two-point conversion to make it 50 to 50 — and to send the game into yet *another* overtime!

By now, both sides were exhausted. But neither was about to give up. The Razorbacks scored another touchdown. Then they made their two-point conversion to take an eight-point lead.

With the game on the line, Manning once more took control. He marched the team down the gridiron, past the 50, into Arkansas territory — *deep* into Arkansas territory. It was fourth down, two to go, at the 6-yard line. Eli chewed up those last six yards with two short passes, both to Jason Armstead, for a record-breaking sixth touchdown pass of the game.

Everyone knew what to expect next. The Rebels had to try for two points. They did, but unfortunately, this time, they failed. As the buzzer sounded the end of the game, Arkansas had 58 points. Ole Miss had 56.

Eli and his teammates were crushed. To have played so well for so long, only to lose in the final moments, was demoralizing. That defeat may have been the reason for their decline in the following weeks. After a rip-roaring season start of six wins to one loss, they dropped two of their last three after the loss to Arkansas to end the season with a 7–4 record. There would be no Bowl game for the Rebels that year.

For his own part, Eli concluded his first season as starting quarterback with some astonishing statistics. In 11 games, he had attempted 408 passes and made 259, 31 of which were good for touchdowns. He had 2,948 passing yards and only nine interceptions. In all, he set 17 school records, including most touchdown passes in a single game. He was presented with the Conerly Trophy, given to Mississippi's top college player, and was a semifinalist for the Davey O'Brien Award, for the nation's top quarterback. He also made *Football News*'s All-America Honors list as an Honorable Mention.

⋆ CHAPTER FOURTEEN ⋆

2002

Junior Glory

With one full year of play under his belt and his background as the son and brother of two great football quarterbacks, it was no surprise that Eli Manning was beginning to be mentioned as a possible Heisman Trophy candidate for 2002. But Archie quickly put an end to that talk. He had seen how much pressure it had caused Peyton and didn't want Eli to go through the same.

Eli agreed. He preferred to focus his efforts on playing to win games, not a trophy.

But winning games didn't turn out to be that simple in 2002, at least not in the second half of the season. After posting five wins in their first six games, Ole Miss lost five in a row.

The problems didn't seem to be with the offense, which behind Eli's direction was racking up high scores in most games. In fact, in the team's first loss, to Texas Tech, Manning beat school records in three categories, including greatest number of 250-yard passing games (9), longest streak of games in which he threw a touchdown pass (15), and most pass attempts (57). The previous holder of that last record? Archie Manning, with 56 in 1970.

Eli was closing in on his father's legacy in other categories, too. He was tied with Archie for 300-yard passing games (three) and just 895 yards shy of his father's career passing yard total of 4,753.

The Rebels managed to win their last regular season game, against its archrival, Mississippi State. The game, known for 75 years by its nickname, the Egg Bowl (after the egg-shaped trophy awarded to the winner), had been won by the Bulldogs for the past five years. But this year, the Golden Egg Trophy returned to Ole Miss, thanks in large part to Eli Manning, who sealed the victory with a one-yard run into the end zone midway through the fourth quarter.

The win was a big morale booster for Manning and his teammates. "After losing [to State] last year, and five losses in a row this year, we really wanted it," Eli said. "We had a lot on the line."

What was on the line was their chance to play in

an official Bowl game. The win over Mississippi State gave them that chance. On December 27, they faced Nebraska in the Independence Bowl.

The Cornhuskers had disappointed their fans by losing seven of their 14 regular season games. But they looked as though they might redeem themselves in this match as their defense delivered a series of blitzes and constant pressure to hold Ole Miss to just seven points as halftime neared. At the same time, they chalked up 17 points of their own.

But then Eli Manning stepped up the Rebels' offensive game. With less than two minutes left in the half, he worked them 88 yards down the field in nine plays. Then he handed off to Toward Sanford, who dove from the 1-yard line into the end zone to bring the score to 17–14.

Although the Cornhuskers managed to get another touchdown in the second half, the final game stats show just how completely the Rebels controlled the field. After allowing the opposing offense 262 yards in the first two quarters, they allowed them to gain just 97 yards in the final two!

Ole Miss took the game, 27–23, to end their season at seven wins, six losses. Manning had been masterful, throwing 25 completions out of 44 attempts for 313 yards. Those numbers earned him the top slot as the school's career passing leader — and heightened rumors that this game would be his last as a college player.

Speculation that Eli Manning would enter the NFL draft as a junior had been running rampant since the beginning of the season. It wasn't surprising. In his two years as the starting quarterback for Ole Miss, he had broken several school records — many set by his father 30 years earlier — and shown the kind of leadership that pro teams look for in their quarterbacks.

Eli, typically, was quiet about his intentions. Unlike Peyton, who had asked advice of several pro athletes when he was considering entering the draft early, Eli preferred to figure things out his own.

"I'll take all the information in, but then sit down and decide myself," he once said. "I don't like people knowing what I'm thinking."

He didn't keep the football world in suspense for long. Two weeks after being named the Most Valuable Offensive Player for his performance in the Independence Bowl, Manning announced that he was returning to Ole Miss to play his senior year.

"I look forward to the 2003 season under Coach Cutcliffe and our staff and to spending another year with my teammates," he told the press, adding that he planned to be a good leader, "so everybody needs to be ready to go to work."

★ CHAPTER FIFTEEN ★

2003

Senior Moments

Eli Manning and the team practiced throughout the spring and into the summer. When they returned to campus in the fall, they were looking to improve on their 7–6 record — and that's exactly what they did.

They won their opener, a close contest against Vanderbilt, 24–21. Manning threw his first TD pass of the season five minutes into the fourth quarter to seal the win. He threw four more in the next game, a heartbreaking 44–34 loss to Memphis that saw Ole Miss giving up 23 points in the fourth quarter.

The Rebels won their third game by a wide margin of 59–14, then lost another high-scoring match to Texas Tech, 49–45. Eli was good that game, going 29 for 49 for 409 yards. Normally, that would have been enough to roll over the opposition with ease. But this game, Texas Tech's quarterback, B.J. Symons, was absolutely awe-inspiring: he completed 44 of 64 attempts for an amazing 661 yards!

Ole Miss was now two and two, with six games remaining in the regular season. Some fans wondered if they would split evenly, as they had in 2002. They got their answer in the next month and a half.

On October 4, Ole Miss beat Florida State 20–17. A week later, they trounced Arkansas 55–0. Ole Miss scored seven touchdowns that day, four of which were passes from the capable hands of Eli Manning. Four more victories followed before the Rebels' winning streak was snapped by a 17–14 loss to Louisiana State University. But there were still two games to be played — and when they were over, Ole Miss had two more hash marks in the "win" column, one of which was a 31–0 pasting of archrival Mississippi State for their second Egg Bowl victory.

The Rebels' regular season ended with that Egg Bowl, but they still had one game left to play: the Cotton Bowl on January 2, 2004. Eli Manning spent December training with the team and receiving several football honors, including the Davey O'Brien Award, the Johnny Unitas Golden Arm Award, the Conerly Award, and the Maxwell Trophy. He also received recognition for his academic achievements and his role as outstanding student-athlete.

Then came the Cotton Bowl. The Rebels of Ole Miss were facing the Cowboys of Oklahoma State. It was the first time since 1991 that Ole Miss was participating in a January Bowl game. Then, they had lost to Michigan in the Gator Bowl — and 20 years before that, they had lost the same game to Auburn. In fact, the last time they'd won a January Bowl was in 1970 when their starting quarterback was none other than Archie Manning.

Going into the Cotton Bowl, Eli owned 45 school records, including 27 that had once belonged to his father. Whatever he did during the game against the Cowboys would only enhance those records, making them even harder to beat by those who followed in his footsteps in the coming years.

But school records weren't on Eli's mind before or during the game. Neither was the fact that many famous professional quarterbacks had once stood where he was about to stand. Joe Montana, Dan Marino, Joe Theismann — all had played and won the Cotton Bowl before going on to NFL fame. But Eli wasn't thinking about them. What was on his mind was winning.

He started off strong with a 16-yard touchdown pass late in the first quarter. Oklahoma evened things up before the quarter ended and then added seven more points four minutes into the second. But Ole Miss answered with seven of their own on a 25-yard

TD pass, and three more besides to take the lead going into halftime. Another touchdown in the third quarter gave them a solid ten-point lead, and yet another in the opening minutes of the fourth seemed to clinch the win.

But then Oklahoma surged back. With 8:50 showing on the game clock, the Cowboys galloped into the end zone to make it 31–21. Four minutes later, they scored again to make it 31–28.

Four minutes is a near-eternity in football time. Mississippi had possession after Oklahoma's second touchdown, but one mistake could easily put the ball back into the Cowboys' hands. All the Cowboys would need to do then was kick a field goal to send the game into overtime.

Eli wasn't about to let that happen. He took command of the field — and not only held it for the remaining four minutes, 38 seconds, but drove the Rebels 85 yards to Oklahoma's 15-yard line just as the clock ran out!

When the buzzer sounded, Eli and his teammates whooped and cheered along with their fans.

"To come to the Cotton Bowl and have your last game with all of those guys and get out a win," Eli said later, "is something I will always remember. It's been a great run."

A great run indeed. Eli Manning finished off his college career with 47 school records, including greatest total passing yards with 10,119, most touchdown passes with 81, most completions with 829, and most attempts with 1,363. He was named the SEC Offensive Player of the Year by the Associated Press and coaches, as well as the first team All-SEC honors. He was third in voting for the Heisman Trophy, too.

Now that his final college game was over, the NFL buzz that had surrounded Eli for months grew to a roar. That Eli was destined to become the third Manning listed in NFL rosters was certain. The question was, which team would pick him — and would he accept the team that did?

★ CHAPTER SIXTEEN ★

2004

Eli the Rookie

The 2004 National Football League draft was scheduled to take place at the end of April. Before then, rumors flew that the San Diego Chargers, who had the first pick that year, were looking very closely at Eli Manning.

Eli had no interest in playing for San Diego, however, for one very simple reason: The Chargers hadn't had a winning season since 1995 and by all accounts were still plagued with major problems. If he played for them, the pressure to turn the team around would be tremendous. Eli knew that better than most because of his own father's experience with the Saints.

Archie agreed that San Diego was not a good place for Eli to begin his professional career. In an effort to dissuade the Chargers from choosing his son, he met with the team's management shortly before the

all thoughts about any discomfort were pushed aside. There was simply too much on the line, for the winner of this game would advance to the Super Bowl.

Favre and the Packers were the sentimental favorites to win. Favre was one of the oldest quarterbacks in the league and one of the most talented. Since he joined the team in 1992, Green Bay had had only one losing season and had gone into the postseason a remarkable ten times. They beat the Patriots in 1996 to become Super Bowl champs and nearly repeated the following year but fell to the Denver Broncos.

Any chance of them adding another Super Bowl ring to their collection ended that frigid January day. The two teams were neck-and-neck throughout the game. 3–0 Giants, 7–6 Packers, 13–10 Giants, 17–13 Packers: the score seesawed back and forth between the two evenly matched teams until finally, it balanced out at 20–20 with two and a half minutes left in the fourth quarter.

Then the Giants got a lucky break. Green Bay fumbled the ball on a punt return and New York recovered at the Packers' 48-yard line. Manning threw a quick shotgun pass to Ahmed Bradshaw. Bradshaw raced down to the end zone for a touchdown!

But before the Giants could celebrate, the officials were whistling them back into position. A penalty flag had been thrown during Bradshaw's run. The penalty was against the Giants. The touchdown was nullified!

If Eli was disappointed, he didn't show it. He simply marched his team down the field into field goal range. Then, with four seconds remaining, he stood back and let the team's kicker, Lawrence Tynes, do his job.

Only Tynes didn't do his job. The kick was wide. The game went into overtime.

The Packers got the ball at the New York 26-yard line. A quick handoff gained them two yards. Good, but not great. Favre tried for a short pass to wide receiver Donald Driver.

The ball never reached Driver because New York's Corey Webster intercepted it and ran it to Green Bay's 34-yard line.

Three downs later, the ball was at the 29. All New York needed was a field goal to win. They were in prime position to get it, if Lawrence Tynes could kick it through the uprights. Given the fact that he had missed his last two, there was no guarantee that he would.

Except this time, he did. With those three points,

the New York Giants won the NFC Championship. They were on their way to the Super Bowl!

"Right now I'm excited as I can be," Manning said after the victory. "We knew we could compete with anybody. It's just a matter of getting hot at the right time."

Brett Favre seconded Manning's trust in the Giants. "Heck, they could win two weeks from now. I wouldn't put it past them."

★ CHAPTER TWENTY ★

2008

Beating the Unbeatable

To no one's surprise, the New England Patriots were also Super Bowl–bound. The team had continued its undefeated season by besting Jacksonville and San Diego by decisive margins. Against their power, the New York Giants were the clear underdogs. Some in the sports media were predicting that the Pats would win by as much as two touchdowns.

Super Bowl XLII took place on February 3, 2008, in Glendale, Arizona. After *American Idol* winner Jordin Sparks opened the game by singing the National Anthem, New York won the toss and elected to receive. The two teams took to the field and readied themselves for the showdown.

Pats kicker Stephen Gostkowski booted the ball 72 yards. Domenik Hixon made the catch and ran the ball to the Giants' 23-yard line. Eli and the New York offense trotted onto the field. It was go time.

And "go" is just what they did — from their 23 to their 42 for first down in three plays. Three plays later they were at New England's 46-yard line. Three more and they were at New England's 37. Three more brought them to the 26, and three more brought them to the 18!

Eli Manning's four first downs on his first drive was a new Super Bowl record — and one that had Patriots' fans openmouthed with disbelief. Their much-touted defense had just allowed the Giants to hold the ball for ten minutes, 15 plays, and 63 yards! And now it looked like New York was going to score!

New York did score, although only a three-point field goal instead of the six-point touchdown and extra point they undoubtedly hoped to have. Still, they had shown New England that, underdog or no, they were playing to win.

But the Patriots were just as eager for victory. Tom Brady responded by working his team down the field. They reached the 17-yard line in front of New York's end zone in five minutes.

With less than a minute remaining in the first quarter, Brady threw to Benjamin Watson in the end zone. Incomplete. Second down and ten to go.

Brady threw to Kevin Faulk. Incomplete. Third down and ten to go.

Brady threw to Watson again. Incomplete!

The Giants' fans leaped to the feet to celebrate — only to sink slowly down again. Antonio Pierce of the Giants had interfered with the pass. It was a costly penalty, one that moved the line of scrimmage to the 1-yard line just as the first quarter ended. To no one's surprise, when the second quarter began, the Patriots scored a touchdown.

Patriots 7, Giants 3.

Disaster struck the Giants again on their next possession. After moving the team into touchdown range, Eli Manning threw an interception, his first in the 2007 postseason.

The Pats took over at their own 33-yard line. Their fans sat back in relief. Surely their team would score again now!

They didn't. Three plays later, New England was forced to punt.

The Giants couldn't do anything either, however — and in fact, when Eli fumbled it looked like the Patriots would reclaim the ball in touchdown range. Fortunately, the Giants recovered, but wound up punting, too.

If New York fans were disappointed by their offense after that mistake, they were cheered by their defense moments later. Packing a powerful one-two punch, Justin Tuck and Kawika Mitchell stopped Laurence Maroney from gaining any yards on his run. On the next play Mitchell broke through and sacked Brady. And on the next, Tuck hurled Brady to the ground! Those back-to-back sacks ended the Patriots' possession with a loss of 14 yards.

Unfortunately for the Giants, Eli was sacked on their next possession, and when Bradshaw was called for illegally batting the ball forward, their touchdown try ended in another punt. They got the ball back after yet another Brady sack ended in a fumble, but the half ran out before they could get into scoring position.

Although the Giants were four points behind the Patriots at halftime, they had reason to celebrate. Their defense had held the best offense in the league to just 81 yards in the first half — and they weren't done yet. In the third quarter, they prevented New England from scoring a single point!

New England returned the favor, however, so going into the final quarter, the score remained Patriots 7, Giants 3. The way the offenses were playing, it looked like this Super Bowl would go down in history for the lowest scores ever.

But the Giants got control. On his first play of the fourth quarter, Eli Manning spiraled a 45-yard pass into hands of Kevin Boss. Three plays later, they were knocking on New England's door — and one play after that, Eli rocketed a short pass that sent that door flying off its hinges. Touchdown! The Giants were in the lead!

There were still 11 minutes to go in the game. The Patriots and the Giants each chewed up one and a half but failed to score. New England took control with eight minutes remaining.

Up until that point, most people agreed that Tom Brady hadn't looked like the winningest quarterback in the league. Now he did. He used a series of short passes to work his team down the field. Five minutes later, he connected with Randy Moss in the end zone. When the extra point was good, the Patriots were up 14 to 10 with less than three minutes left to play. If New England's defense could stop Eli Manning, the Patriots would walk away with a Super Bowl victory — their fourth in six years — and the only perfect season in NFL history.

But New England's defense couldn't stop Manning. First he connected with Toomer on a short pass for a gain of 11. Three plays and two incomplete passes later, he found Toomer again for nine yards. With the game on the line and only a yard to go for first down, the Giants decided to risk a fourth-down play. Their risk paid off thanks to a 2-yard run by Jacobs.

A minute and a half remained as the teams set up at the Giants' 44-yard line. Manning tried for a shotgun pass only to see the Patriots' defense surge toward him. Somehow, he managed to avoid them — and scramble for five yards!

His next pass was incomplete, but the one after connected for a crucial 32-yard gain. The Giants were in scoring range at New England's 24!

The Patriots weren't about to hand over the game, however. They sacked Eli Manning on the next play for a loss of one. They denied him any gain on the next attempt, too, an incomplete pass intended for David Tyree.

And then came the play that ended it all. With one minute, 15 seconds to go, the Giants were at their own 44-yard line. Eli Manning took the snap and faded back for a pass.

The Patriots' defense surrounded him. They clutched his shirt. They pulled at him.

Somehow, Eli remained on his feet. And those feet moved, taking him away from those tacklers and into an open spot where he was free to throw. Cool as a cucumber, he launched a 32-yard pass toward Tyree.

Giants and Patriots fans held their breath. Tyree jumped and found the ball. It was one of the most bizarre catches ever, for Tyree caught the ball against his helmet, pressed it there, and held it despite being mauled by tacklers!

That catch, made at the New England 24, was all the advantage Giants needed. True, Eli was sacked for a loss of a yard. True, his next pass was incomplete. But the one after was good — and the one after that was outstanding, a 13-yard bullet into the hands of his favorite receiver, Plaxico Burress, whose feet just happened to be planted in New England's end zone!

Touchdown! The Giants were in the lead 17–14, with less than a minute remaining in the game!

The Patriots mounted the best assault they could, but the Giants' defense denied them completely. Pass incomplete. Sack. Pass incomplete. And another incomplete pass gave the Giants the ball on the New England 16-yard line with one second left to play.

Eli Manning used that second wisely. He took the snap and, game ball in hand, knelt down on the turf. The Giants had beaten the unbeatable Patriots!

Eli was swarmed by his teammates. Plaxico Burress burst into tears of joy. David Tyree called Manning a shining leader. Coach Tom Coughlin, usually stony-faced, was all smiles.

In a luxury box high above the field, the previous year's Super Bowl MVP, Peyton Manning, leaped, cheered, and pumped his fists. "The scramble will go down as one of the greatest plays of all time," he predicted.

Archie and Olivia celebrated in another booth nearby. "I couldn't be prouder," Archie said. "I never thought about them [Peyton and Eli] even playing college ball, much less pro football, much less winning Super Bowls."

Cooper, the joker of the family who had once said he'd have a whole handful of Super Bowl rings if he'd been able to keep playing, was overjoyed for his brother. But as usual, he tempered his praise with a playful jab by saying, "How hard can it be to win the Super Bowl?"

Plenty hard was the answer, of course. New England players and fans were stunned. "How? How had it happened?" they asked themselves.

Eli had a simple reply to that question: "We played better than they did."

Super Bowl fans and the sports media clearly thought Manning had played better than anyone else on the field. They awarded him MVP, making it the second time in two years that the name Manning had been etched on that trophy and earning Peyton and Eli a place in NFL history as the only brothers to win back-to-back Super Bowls as well as back-to-back Super Bowl MVP awards.

☆ EPILOGUE ☆

With the Super Bowl XLII victory, Eli took his place alongside Peyton and Archie as an equal member of the greatest football family in NFL history. The Mannings' dominance on the field is indisputable and will likely extend for many years to come. Yet it is what they do off the field that elevates them above some of their peers.

The Manning family has a long history of helping others and giving back to their communities. Archie organizes and plays in charity golf tournaments aimed at raising money for cystic fibrosis research and to support the Salvation Army and Boy Scouts. He has also helped out with the Louisiana Special Olympics and United Way.

Peyton established his own charitable organization, the PeyBack Foundation, in 1999, with the goal of helping disadvantaged children by supporting youth programs in Indiana, Tennessee, and

Louisiana. The Foundation distributes donations to summer athletics programs, food banks, and youth clubs; it also sponsors special events around the holidays and organizes football tournaments among inner-city teams. More recently, Peyton gave his name to the children's wing of Indianapolis's St.Vincent hospital.

Just how important helping others is to the Mannings became clear after Hurricane Katrina devastated the Mannings' hometown of New Orleans in late August of 2005. Within days, Peyton and Eli had mobilized their own relief efforts, filling a plane with much needed supplies and repeatedly offering their assistance in any way they could.

"I talked to the Red Cross," Peyton said, "and told them I certainly didn't want to get in the way, but I wanted to do whatever I could to help."

"It's hard to watch what's happened to the city, people with no place to go, up to their waists in water," Eli added, his face grim. "We just wanted to do something extra, so we set up this plan to help some of these people."

Eli has helped in other ways, too. In 2006, he took part in a massive hunger relief effort called Feed the Children. He helped raise nearly 2.5 million dollars for a new state-of-the-art wing for the University of

Mississippi's children's hospital. "My dad. . . . never said that my brothers, Cooper and Peyton, and I had to do anything [for others]," Eli once said, "but that if we did, we should do it for the right reasons. Because if you're not excited about what you're doing, it's not going to do much good."

This sentiment, to be excited about what one's doing, seems to be the Manning motto. Sure, Cooper may wish his youngest brother would show his excitement more obviously. Eli may wish his middle brother didn't show it so dramatically. And Peyton and Eli may wish that their oldest brother had had a chance to show it on the gridiron with them.

But no matter what has happened in the past or what the future holds, one thing is for certain — whenever either Manning quarterback takes to the field, something exciting is bound to happen. And when it does, no one will be cheering louder than the members of the Manning clan, the number-one family in professional football.

Peyton Manning's NFL Statistics

Regular Season

Stats	Team	G	GS	PASSING												RUSHING				FUMBLES	
				COMP	ATT	PCT	YDS	YD/ATT	LNG	TD	INT	SCK	SCK YDS	RTG	ATT	YDS	AVG	TD	FUM	LOST
1998	Colts	16	16	326	575	56.7	3,739	6.5	78	26	28	22	109	71.2	15	62	4.1	0	3	1
1999	Colts	16	16	331	533	62.1	4,135	7.8	80	26	15	14	116	90.7	35	73	2.1	2	6	3
2000	Colts	16	16	357	571	62.5	4,413	7.7	78	33	15	20	131	94.7	37	116	3.1	1	5	2
2001	Colts	16	16	343	547	62.7	4,131	7.6	86	26	23	29	232	84.1	35	157	4.5	4	7	3
2002	Colts	16	16	392	591	66.3	4,200	7.1	69	27	19	23	145	88.8	38	148	3.9	2	6	2
2003	Colts	16	16	379	566	67.0	4,267	7.5	79	29	10	18	107	99.0	28	26	0.9	0	6	1
2004	Colts	16	16	336	497	67.6	4,557	9.2	80	49	10	13	101	121.1	25	38	1.5	0	5	1
2005	Colts	16	16	305	453	67.3	3,747	8.3	80	28	10	17	81	104.1	33	45	1.4	0	5	2
2006	Colts	16	16	362	557	65.0	4,397	7.9	68	31	9	14	86	101.0	23	36	1.6	4	2	1
2007	Colts	16	16	337	515	65.4	4,040	7.8	73	31	14	21	124	98.0	20	-5	-0.3	3	6	1
Career		160	160	3,468	5,405	64.2	41,626	7.7	86	306	153	191	1,232	94.7	289	696	2.4	16	51	17

Postseason

Stats	Team	G	GS	PASSING											RUSHING				FUMBLES	
				COMP	ATT	PCT	YDS	YD/ATT	LNG	TD	INT	SCK	SCK YDS	RTG	ATT	YDS	AVG	TD	FUM	LOST
1998	Colts	16	16	326	575	56.7	3,739	6.5	78	26	28	22	109	71.2	15	62	4.1	0	3	1
1999	Colts	1	1	19	42	45.2	227	5.4	33	0	0	0	0	62.3	3	22	7.3	1	0	0
2000	Colts	1	1	17	32	53.1	194	6.1	30	1	0	0	0	82.0	1	-2	-2.0	0	0	0
2002	Colts	1	1	14	31	45.2	137	4.4	17	0	2	1	13	31.2	1	2	2.0	0	0	0
2003	Colts	3	3	67	103	65.0	918	8.9	87	9	4	5	41	106.4	4	3	0.8	0	1	0
2004	Colts	2	2	54	75	72.0	696	9.3	49	4	2	2	12	107.4	2	8	4.0	1	1	0
2005	Colts	1	1	22	38	57.9	290	7.6	50	1	0	5	43	90.9	0	0	-	0	0	0
2006	Colts	4	4	97	153	63.4	1,034	6.8	52	3	7	6	41	70.5	8	3	0.4	1	1	1
2007	Colts	1	1	33	48	68.8	402	8.4	55	3	2	0	0	97.7	1	-6	-6.0	0	0	0
Career		14	14	323	522	61.9	3,898	7.5	87	21	17	19	150	84.6	20	30	1.5	3	3	1

Eli Manning's NFL Statistics

Regular Season

Stats	Team	G	GS	PASSING											RUSHING				FUMBLES	
				COMP	ATT	PCT	YDS	YD/ATT	LNG	TD	INT	SCK	SCK YDS	RTG	ATT	YDS	AVG	TD	FUM	LOST
2004	Giants	9	7	95	197	48.2	1,043	5.3	52	6	9	13	83	55.4	6	35	5.8	0	3	1
2005	Giants	16	16	294	557	52.8	3,762	6.8	78	24	17	28	184	75.9	29	80	2.8	1	9	2
2006	Giants	16	16	301	522	57.7	3,244	6.2	55	24	18	25	186	77.0	25	21	0.8	0	9	2
2007	Giants	16	16	297	529	56.1	3,336	6.3	60	23	20	27	217	73.9	29	69	2.4	1	13	7
Career		57	55	987	1,805	54.7	11,385	6.3	78	77	64	93	670	73.4	89	205	2.3	2	34	12

Postseason

Stats	Team	G	GS	PASSING											RUSHING				FUMBLES	
				COMP	ATT	PCT	YDS	YD/ATT	LNG	TD	INT	SCK	SCK YDS	RTG	ATT	YDS	AVG	TD	FUM	LOST
2005	Giants	1	1	10	18	55.6	113	6.3	0	0	3	4	22	35.0	0	0	-	0	1	1
2006	Giants	1	1	16	27	59.3	161	6.0	29	2	1	1	7	85.6	2	4	2.0	0	0	0
2007	Giants	4	4	72	119	60.5	854	7.2	52	6	1	9	47	95.7	8	10	1.3	0	2	0
Career		6	6	98	164	59.8	1,128	6.9	52	8	5	14	76	84.1	10	14	1.4	0	3	1

Peyton Manning's Year-to-Year NFL Highlights

1998:
- First round draft pick overall
- Breaks rookie records for:
    Most passes attempted (575)
    Most passes completed (326)
    Most yards gained (3,739)
    Most touchdown passes (26)
    Most consecutive games with a touchdown (13)
- NFL All-Rookie First Team

1999:
- Selected to play in Pro Bowl
- Second Team All-Pro

2000:
- Selected to play in Pro Bowl
- Second Team All-Pro

2002:
- Selected to play in Pro Bowl

2003:
- Co-NFL MVP (with Steve McNair)
- Bert Bell Award

- First Team All-Pro
- Selected to play in Pro Bowl

2004:
- NFL MVP
- Bert Bell Award
- Best NFL Player ESPY Award
- Selected to play in Pro Bowl
- First Team All-Pro
- AFC Player of the Year

2005:
- Best NFL Player ESPY Award
- Best Record-Breaking Performance ESPY Award
- Walter Payton Man of the Year Award
- Selected to play in Pro Bowl
- Pro Bowl MVP
- Byron "Whizzer" White Humanitarian Award
- First Team All-Pro

2006:
- Selected to play in Pro Bowl
- Second Team All-Pro

2007:
- Member of the Super Bowl Championship Team
- Super Bowl MVP

- Best Championship Performance ESPY Award
- Selected to play in Pro Bowl

Eli Manning's Year-to-Year NFL Highlights

2004:
- First round draft pick overall

2008:
- Member of the Super Bowl Championship Team
- Super Bowl MVP